Cognitive Distortions

How to catch the Top Ten
Most Dangerous Thinking Villains

Written by

Gaelle Carey and Danielle Ritenour

Illustrated by Nicole DeCoster, Claujia Fayniko R. and Becca Ritenour

For information regarding permission, please write to:
info@barringerpublishing.com
Barringer Publishing, Naples, Florida
www.barringerpublishing.com

Layout Design by Linda S. Duider
Cape Coral, Florida

ISBN: 978-1-954396-28-9

Library of Congress Cataloging-in-Publication Data
Gaelle Carey and Danielle Ritenour
*Cognitive Distortions: How to Catch the Top Ten
Most Dangerous Thinking Villains*
cognitivedistortionsbook.com

Printed in the U.S.A.

TABLE OF CONTENTS

FOREWORD

Dear Mental Health Professional,

As a mental health professional, you have committed your time, resources, energy, and mental and emotional capacities in support of the social and emotional needs of clients. Your work is valuable and critical for the well-being of our communities and society.

You likely chose this profession due to your sense of inequity and communal well-being, possibilities for healing and resiliency, a desire to nurture environments of safety and introspection, and to the care of others. While the work can offer a great deal of fulfillment and intrinsic reward, it's not long before many mental health professionals are also confronted with the sobering realities of the work.

The work you engage in can be complex, taxing, and involves the navigation of many workplace environments, healthcare settings, and client demographics needs. At times, it can feel as if you are stuck in the middle of competing priorities between providing quality client care and meeting the logistical demands of your therapeutic context. In the midst of all this, you are likely to have a desire for professional development as you strive to support clients and their loved ones. While some mental health professionals have access to professional support and guidance, this too can be more the exception than the rule in overtaxed mental health systems. It can, oftentimes, feel like an impossible task to know how to proceed in the face of these dynamics and can lead to professionals feeling burnt out, dissatisfied, and discontent with the work and themselves because you feel compelled to make compromises.

While the field has made tremendous strides in understanding the unique developmental aspects of children and their social and emotional needs, the field of psychotherapy has basically emanated from engagement with adults. While well-intended, many training programs and workplace contexts continue to focus on training mental health professionals from this adult-centric stance, with the goal of extrapolating this to the needs of children and their family systems. As a mental health professional working with children, this can lead to many questions, feelings of incompetence in our work with children and the adults in their lives, and can further reinforce and complicate the aforementioned challenges.

It is with firsthand knowledge of your work as well as what your daily environment may feel like, that this book has been written as a resource and support medium. No matter your background, education, training, or current therapeutic context, *Cognitive Distortions* can provide you with a practical source of guidance as you work to support the mental health needs of children and their families and caregivers.

Danielle Ritenour and Gaelle Carey are both licensed mental health providers with years of experience with children, working to support their mental health needs as well as their families' requirements. From their training and applied experience working in community-based systems to the larger technology-based, healthcare settings, Danielle and Gaelle have the nuanced knowledge of child mental health care to provide tailored support for clinicians as they engage in this important and challenging work with children.

This book, *Cognitive Distortions,* offers mental health professionals knowledge and concepts applicable to children that is based on evidence and research-based work. It is then applied tactfully to the needs of children. Danielle and Gaelle have diligently drawn from and worked to translate the concepts of cognitive behavioral therapy in a way that can be accessed and made relatable to children. In a very conversational manner, the book offers practical insights and options for supporting the needs of children and helping them better understand brain function and to work with themselves in a way that promotes healthy thinking patterns and coping strategies. The colorful drawings throughout the book will feel approachable, congruent with children, and help further engagement with the material you decide to apply. For older children, the book could even become a useful resource in that they can turn to themselves and utilize with the support of their caregivers.

Cognitive Distortions is a valuable resource for any mental health professional working to support children, regardless of your experience and level of comfort in childcare. The book can be quickly referenced and utilized as a more immediate resource and can also provide a potential longer term path and plan to address the many intersecting components of the mental health journey for children. Children will be supported in the utilization of evidence-based techniques as well as understanding these concepts in a way that makes sense to them and such techniques can be practically applied.

It is with knowledge, experience, and passion that Danielle and Gaelle offer this compilation for the edification of the mental health professional striving to support the needs of children and their caregivers. May this resource offer you a sense of reassurance and hope as you navigate complex mental systems while striving to keep the child and their needs at the center of your work and efforts.

Tyler J. Cole
Licensed Mental Health Professional

ACKNOWLEDGMENTS

. . . .

"When you touch one thing with deep awareness, you touch everything."

~ THICH NHAT HANH

We dedicate this book to all people who experience negative thinking patterns—you are worthy of being happy and loved. We give a special thanks to Aaron Beck, who is considered the father of cognitive behavior therapy and passed away November 1, 2021.

Danielle gives a special dedication to her grandma who was well-loved and dealt with mental health issues for a large portion of her life and still kept a smile on her face. Danielle also wants to dedicate this book to her three nephews, Roy, Robert, and Mateo who provide endless joy; we may live across the country, but I enjoy the time we get when we see each other.

Gaelle gives a special dedication to her mother Nicole who is her source of inspiration, wisdom, and knowledge. This work is also dedicated to her father

Didier, whose good examples have taught her to work hard for the things that she aspires to achieve. Also, to her husband, Dave, who has constantly encouraged Gaelle and stood by her side. Gaelle also gives gratitude to her siblings, children and grandchildren for their unwavering support.

INTRODUCTION

Dear Reader,

We are very happy that you have decided to be proactive about your mental health. Talking about mental health has been a taboo topic for too long. Our *Cognitive Distortions: How to Catch the Top Ten Thinking Villains* was created with mental health providers and families in mind.

The authors acknowledge that these last few years have brought up a lot of uncertainty. We want to make sure that parents and mental health providers have clear and understandable ways to talk about negative thinking patterns with kids and amongst themselves.

The authors, Gaelle Carey and Danielle Ritenour, are licensed marriage and family therapists who have been practicing for over five years. They have noticed common themes with their clients in therapy and particularly during the pandemic over these past two years, demonstrating a need for more skilled mental health providers on the ground.

Gaelle and Danielle both hope that the stories in this book will encourage new and safe ways to talk about mental health without the stigmas that accompany it. Negative thinking patterns are commonly seen in everyday communication and human interaction.

This book is intended to raise awareness about these commonly occurring negative thinking patterns with the hope that this knowledge will encourage our readers to talk more kindly about themselves. The stories in this volume can be read by the whole family as well as in schools and therapy practices. These fun short stories are designed to help the reader understand where anxiety comes from and how everyday acts and thoughts can help reduce those anxieties.

We cannot solve our problems with the same thinking we used when we created them.

~ ALBERT EINSTEIN

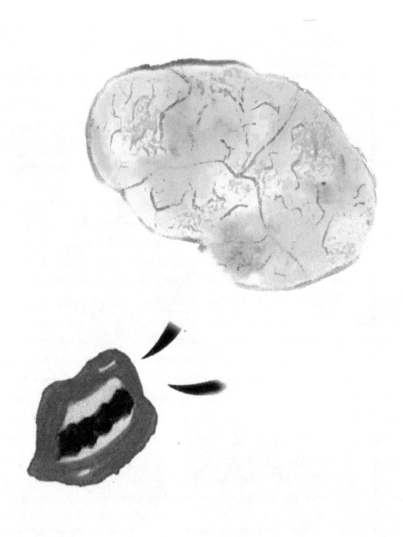

Who are the Cognitive Distortion Villains: What are they and why are they called thinking villains?

The Mighty Brain

Once upon a time there was the **Almighty Brain** who sat in a head and said:

> "I am a squiggly, jiggly blob and I am not corn on the cob. I am one of the biggest wonders known, like a planet on a throne."

Oh, how the Mighty Brain is so pinkish-greyish; no one would ever believe its complete greatness.

One day, the Mighty Brain noticed their wrinkles becoming crinkled and said:

"This is no tickle, I am feeling somewhat crippled."

The Mighty Brain soon heard a voice, "Peculiar," it said. "I wonder what the source is?"

Over here a noise said: "Nice to meet you, my name is Voice. Who are you?"

I am known as a thought. I release electric signals inside neighboring neurons by sending and receiving messages. I have brought you prompt communication to tell you, Mighty Brain, you have the choice to keep the thought thinking villains away so lets rejoice!

Mighty Brain said: "Who are they, and where are these thinking villains today?"

Thinking villains are called cognitive distortions. They are cognitive tendencies for the way you understand and perceive your surroundings through thinking and they are also called thoughts. These distortions can create inaccurate misrepresentations of reality. It's misleading don't you think?

"Thoughts that are distorted can happen in your head," the Voice said.

"All stinkin ten and they are not real friends; instead, they are known as villains of these cognitive distortions, and they can start quite the commotion."

The Mighty Brain asked:

"Wait, wait, my friend, are these the same ten, the most dangerous crooks, I heard stories about in many different books? The ones that will cause havoc and send people through lots of panic?"

"Well, you see, Mighty Brain," Voice said, "most noggins need oxygen, rest and play; however, sometimes because of feelings like Anger and Fear, things that you care about can seem to easily disappear, and we can find ourselves lost in different parts of the brain not knowing how to get back here where it is safe to come out and play. Cognitive distortions will make you feel worried and sad," Voice said.

"These stinking villains can be found all around, in different small towns, downtowns, and in most suburbs, like the city called Amygdala where villains are known by name and show no pity or remorse when using force."

Wheel of Emotions

You can use the emotional wheel to help you better understand how you feel and learn emotional language.

Voice told the Mighty Brain, in Amygdala, these dangerous thinking villains take any opportunity to use manipulative motions and hijack your emotions. The Mighty Brain was intrigued and wanted to understand more about how to stop difficult feelings of despair from ever reappearing. The Mighty Brain said:

> "Well, go ahead, Voice, tell me each of their names so I can begin to implement a plan and pass on punitive charges to each fugitive."

Voice replied:

> "You're on the right track, Mighty Brain, let me properly introduce you to the Cognitive Distortion (the CD gang), but first let me explain what remains for you to know, so you will be successful on the go."

The prefrontal cortex (PFC) is the front part of the frontal lobes of the brain. It lies in front of the motor and premotor areas.

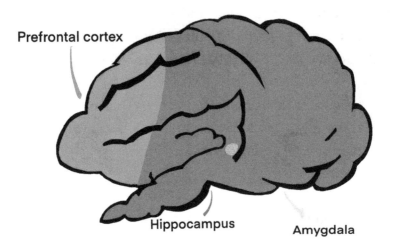

This brain region helps plan complex cognitive behaviors, character expression, and decision making. It helps correct social and emotional behavior. The basic activity of this brain region is to bring together thoughts and actions to help achieve internal needs.

A threat vs a perceived threat

"You see, it's quite easy," said the Voice.

"Most are not told about the superpower that each of the Mighty Brains behold. Life is filled with situations which are only perceived circumstances of how we organize and interpret all kinds of incoming information."

Voice went on to say that when any situation arises, we find ourselves in a space where we have a choice to take a step back before we react. This is known as one of the superpower ingredients called mindfulness, where you shift the gear and idle and where the mind finds complete stillness. Sometimes, things can be really scary because of a real threat like losing your canary. Yet, sometimes, threats are only perceived and appear extreme and ill-conceived.

The Voice asked the Mighty Brain:

> "Do you know how to use the power of mindfulness and not perceive threats unless it's a real threat in the immediate situation."

The Mighty brain said:

> "I am not really sure, is there a cure?"

"Yes," the Voice said.

> "All you have to do is ask yourself one important but simple question, and the question is this: Are you really in true danger right this second?"

The Mighty Brain said:

> "I guess something could happen; I could fall and hurt myself, or even lose my mind, or drive too fast and get a fine."

The Voice said:

> "Yes, of course all those things can happen, but the question is are these things happening to you right now?"

"No," the Mighty Brain said.

> "Then why worry," said the Voice, "and have to stop our fun too early?"

"You're right," said the Mighty Brain. "If I become worried or scared, ask myself first if there is a real threat, but if not, then go get help. If no threat, use mindfulness. I think using mindfulness is really going to help me through this mission and finally stop with all the superstition."

The vagus nerve express

Mighty Brain, did you know that you are the sum of three parts of the whole.

> "The nervous system is the reason I have come this season to help catch these naughty villains so we can rest and digest."

The Voice shouted:

> "Brainy, this may come as a surprise; you hold the key to the control center of the military where you connect to motor nerves that will carry our important messages by traveling through the spinal chord's highway terminal."

The Mighty Brain wanted to know more about the different paths called nerves so it could miss all of the uncomfortable curves.

The Voice reported:

> "Where we are standing right now is the ventral vagal valley, where everyone who resides here is staying connected, feeling safe, relaxed and utilizing communication to get their needs met. Most of us here never take in a situation as a perceived threat or even a real threat for that matter. Here in the ventral valley part of the brain, it is smooth sailing because the waves are just right. Here, thoughts know there is a solution to most situations and most things in life, and through connecting with others and learning how to set limits, we can stay in ventral vagal.

> "The next nerve path, in amygdala, which continues down, mates to the sympathetic nervous system interstate. This is the CD's home address where the aggressive, unimpressive, defensive thinking villains lay. When traveling here, you may feel that your breathing becomes shallow and

your heart beats faster, while you become clammy and quickly start to mobilize the body."

"Why?" said the Mighty Brain?

Once you spend time engaging with the CD gang, you will need to run as fast as you can from the threats perceived, and, consequently, different organs in the body are sent specific messages to shut down transmission.

Finally Voice said:

"If you find fight or flight and have to react rather than act, then be careful. It could be a sign of not reading the right signals and finding yourself heading towards a dead end—down the dorsal vagal road. If you end up on that path, you must listen to me closely, since only one thing can prevent you from shutting down and staying immobilized."

The Mighty Brain said, "I can see how staying on this turnpike too long can be an excessive and a depressing choice."

What is Fight, Flight, Freeze and Fawn?

Your fight, flight freeze or fawn reaction is a tool that you use to protect yourself from danger.

> **Fight:** facing any perceived threat aggressively.

> **Flight:** running away from the danger.

> **Freeze:** unable to move or act against a threat.

> **Fawn:** immediately acting to try to please to avoid any conflict.

Some body responses to your fight or flight response are becoming dizzy or lightheaded, sweating, shaking, difficulty concentrating, tense muscles, heart racing, racing thoughts, and butterflies in the stomach. Which fight, flight, freeze, or fawn response would you have used in the situations provided below:

Getting up in front of your class to recite a poem? Your class singing happy birthday to you during lunch?

Your parents are coming home and you broke your brother's favorite toy?

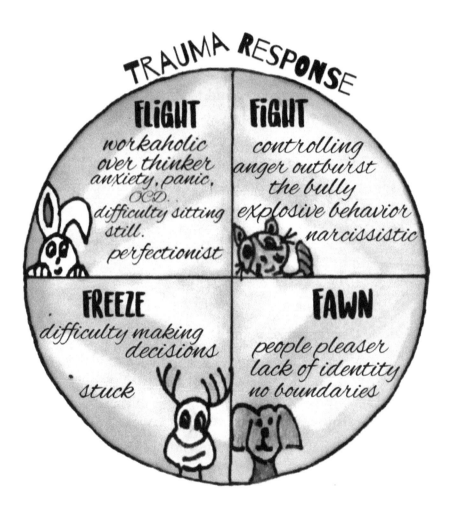

ABCDE Module: Catching those villains with a reframe tool

When we have inaccurate information about our thoughts, sometimes our response can be bigger than we want, leading to regret later and feeling mad and jealous. Sometimes, it's hard because we don't see how things even connect.

The ABCDE coaching model is an approach that helps with thinking more clearly and keeps the cognitive distortion villains at bay. It has five stages:

1. Activating an event or situation.
2. Beliefs
3. Consequences
4. Discrepancies about the beliefs; and
5. Effective new ways of dealing with the problem.

A	Activating Event	I failed a test
B	Initial Beliefs	I am a failure
C	Consequences	What is the point of studying?
D	Discrepancies	I have passed many other tests
E	Effective New Belief	I need to study more/ differently, ask for help

*"There is nothing either good or
bad, but thinking makes it so."*

~ WILLIAM SHAKESPEARE

Polarized or Black and White Thinking

Layla and Kayla

Layla was from the north; she liked to dance and sway back and forth. Kayla was from the south and she was anything but quiet with her big mouth. From far away, one could say these girls were polar opposites. It wasn't hard to see the division that separated them.

Layla liked the color yellow, butterflies, bright tie-dye, and was introverted and mellow. Kayla was not like Layla. She considered herself to be an extrovert, enjoying the shades of blues and hues, funky shoes, and wacky hairdos.

Layla enjoyed reading, writing, and doing different projects with fashion and art. Kayla instead would be making scientific podcasts, and advocating for others from her heart. These were only small aspects that drew these ladies apart with enough of a distinction to bring unwanted division. Both girls were traveling in two opposed directions. Layla identified herself as a vegetarian and wanted to become the world's best veterinarian. Kayla, on the other hand, is a pescatarian and hopes to one day be the first out of space planetarian. Either way, one could say there is no way that these two could come together for a day. Their differences created a paradox in this particular situation.

One day, Layla was sent to detention for drawing on walls and getting a lot of the public's attention. Kayla was already there, didn't look like she gave a care, with her pink, bubblegum-colored hair.

Kayla yelled out to Layla:

> "Are you here because of a dare or your own artistic flare? I must share, I love your art, I must declare."

Layla nearly fell off her chair. She didn't know Kayla even knew she existed or cared. Whatever came next, Layla thought, would be extremely twisted since Kayla had a reputation of being a phenomenal bass-playing

punk rocker, moonwalker and methodical smooth talker.
Layla finally said: "Hey," as she looked Kayla's way.

Kayla asked:

> "Layla, could you make posters, signs and
> banners. Excuse my lack of manners, but
> with your artwork we need your talent
> and skills. There is going to be a protest for
> animal rights and the march was starting at
> the school straight up towards Capital Hills.
> Would you be interested in helping the
> animals, even if it was just for the thrills?
> We want to stop the fashion industry and
> the unnecessary kills."

Layla was surprised. This girl from the South had
something in common without a doubt. Layla did not
think her thoughts were so negative, but now she knew
that thinking in absolutes changed her vision to black
and white thinking. It made her pout.

This could occur completely since choosing black and
white thinking has no place when using free-thinking.
How could some punk rocker have any similar beliefs, let
alone want or need Layla to help her?

Of course, she was all in, and wanted to help out.
There was a great turn out. Everyone at the march held
banners, signs, and posters as they were about to walk

down the selected route. The march went great and many people signed the ballots to help and protect the endangered rhinos.

Who knew such polar opposite girls, could come together, and use their skills like no other. Layla and Kayla were able to meet on a middle ground between two points of view.

Layla said: "It's not easy to see others without any different shades."

That's right Layla! Black and white thinking styles can prevent people from being aware of the full range of colors of their own potentials and possibilities available to them. If we hadn't run into each other, we would have continued with that stinking thinking—or black and white thinking without giving each other a chance to work together.

We hope this helps next time you and a friend argue. Now, you know, your relationship can pull through. You don't have to feel blue.

Why your brain will start sinking when using black and white thinking?

Black and white thinking is a way for the brain to protect you from slipping in-between the cracks. Thinking rigidly can be helpful in an emergency and if experiencing a real threat. However, it doesn't help very much when you're just trying to make it through a tough day.

How to stop black and white thinking villains by thinking in shades of gray

Scaling principle

Instead of seeing people, places and things in absolutes and extremes—whether good or bad, tall or short, skinny or fat, mean or nice, or dumb or smart, first ask yourself, . . . *am I unwilling to see shades of gray? Am I rigid and inflexible?* This method is inadvisable for a happy ending. *Or, am I thinking in shades of gray and mixing black and white in various proportions?*

Next time, when considering any given situation, I want you to think and evaluate things from a range of 1-100 when things don't work out just as you hoped. Now, think about the situation as a partial success instead of a complete failure, and you will be on your way to feeling better. For example, you may say to yourself, *I have to be the best dancer, or I can not dance at all.*

When you look with shades of gray

Defining your terms principle

When you label things, or even yourself, as a failure or anything else, ask yourself, *What is the definition of a failure?* You will feel better when you see that there is no such thing as a person being a 'failure.'

Test yourself on how well you know whether or not you are engaging using black-and-white polarized thinking . . .

1. You've thought: *I am a total failure.*

2. You've thought about the worst that can happen when you're afraid.

3. You believe that you are totally safe driving in your car, or you are a dangerous driver. There is no in-between.

4. You entered a race and lost, and you feel happy that you tried even if you did not win.

Answers: 1. Yes, 2. Yes, 3. Yes, 4. No

Using "And" instead of "But," you can be two things at once principle

We use the word "but" to join things together and to show contrast. However, the word "but," ends up ending the connection. Instead, you should try and use the word "and" to see better harmony between concepts.

Whenever you're about to use the word "but," use the word "and" instead. Remember you can show two things which seem to be opposites at the same time.

For example, one can say "I am confident, and I am sensitive," or "I love you, and I am mad at you."

Let's examine how using the word "and" creates a better connection while using the word "but" creates disconnection.

For example:

> "I am doing the best I can, but I can try harder."

The first part of the sentence ("I am doing the best") becomes unimportant after the word "but" is added. Instead you should say: "I am doing the best I can and I can try harder." That is a much more powerful sentence and statement in general.

Using 'But'

In the following example when Kayla says to Layla:

> "Layla, you made a good poster "but" I know you still can improve with the colors."

Layla may tune Kayla out and become defensive as soon as she hears the modifying word "but" when Kayla comments on Layla's poster for the animal rights march. The modifying word "but" conveys a negative message about the need for Layla to further improve her efforts.

Using 'And' principle

If instead, Kayla says to Layla:

> "Layla you made a good poster 'and' I know you can improve with the colors."

This makes it easier for Kayla to let Layla know what she needs in a positive way and expressing this in a favorable light. Other examples which successfully use the conjunction "and" include the following statements:

1. I feel guilty buying myself a new purse, and I'm still going to buy one.
2. I did really well in the play, and I totally missed two lines.
3. I don't want to go to school, and I can still show up today.

Facts or opinions principle

Sometimes cognitive distortions, those testy thinking villains, can make it hard to know what is real and what is not. When you express an opinion, you are expressing your emotions or feelings which are not likely difficult to prove or disprove. Opinions are subjective, personal views based upon your own interpretation of your current reality. On the other hand, facts can be refuted or validated and supported by evidence . . .

Test yourself on how well you know the difference between facts and opinions.

1. I failed my test.

2. I am five feet six inches.

3. I am smart.

4. I am happy.

5. I want to be a doctor when I grow up.

6. I am taller than then my brother.

7. No one could like me.

8. They can never be nice only mean.

Answers: 1. Fact, 2. Fact, 3. Opinion, 4. Opinion, 5. Fact, 6. Fact 7. Opinion, 8. Opinion

Opposites quiz

1. Short	A. Leader
2. Happy	B. Idle
3. Straight	C. Sad
4. Large	D. Quiet
5. Scared	E. Sleepy
6. Energetic	F. Squiggle
7. Specific	G. Fast
8. Follower	H. Tall
9. Slow	I. Clean
10. Hairy	J. Brave
11. Busy	K. General
12. Messy	L. Bald
13. Loud	M. Tiny

Answers: 1H, 2C, 3F, 4M, 5J, 6E, 7K, 8A, 9G, 10L, 11B, 12I, 13D

"Nothing can stop the man with the right mental attitude from achieving his goal; nothing on earth can help the man with the wrong mental attitude."

~ THOMAS JEFFERSON

Mental Filtering

Caleb

Caleb was not having a good day. It was one of those mornings where the sky was gray. His room was in a complete disarray. He had rent he needed to pay, and while finishing laundry, he found twenty dollars, but the match to his sock went astray. There was traffic so he was late for work.

He enjoyed his job at a famous hotel where he was a desk clerk. Meeting new people everyday, he would always ask where they were from and how long they planned to stay.

Today was not his day though. It was very busy and this couple came in arguing and putting on quite the show. The anger between them rose like bread dough.

Caleb spoke up and shouted:

> "Please, if you are going to put on this display, go outside until your anger is at bay. This is a place where business people come on holiday and need none of this delay."

The couple at once apologized. They checked into the hotel and acted more civilized.

Caleb became wide-eyed! He realized he just yelled at two famous musicians he idolized!

They said:

"Yes, we have been traveling for months."

Because they were on tour; the constant time changes were more than they could endure.

They said sorry for causing such a mess and putting the guests in distress. They would give Caleb Backstage passes. They assured him the concert was already sold out by the masses.

Caleb thought, *Finally, good things are heading my way. I can go to a party and play.*

Right then, his manager called and stated he would have to work late. Why was everything doomed—it was his ultimate fate!

Caleb ended up calling his best friend Kate; she would be able to go and bring a date. He got off work, still mad about missing the concert. He was upset and emotionally hurt. He screamed: "This day is the worst. Why do I feel like I am under a curse!"

When Caleb came home, he saw Kate emerge from the shadow. Kate stated that the concert ended some time ago. Kate wanted to thank him and gave him a personalized signed guitar. Caleb was very surprised and asked: "Why, this is the greatest gift by far!"

Kate stated she knew he was having a hard day, but also pointed out the positives. I want to show you that yes, your day was pretty bad, but one shouldn't only

focus on the negatives. The week's worth of laundry was complete, the house was clean and all neat. Caleb had found a twenty dollar bill and for many that's a big deal and they would want that superior skill.

Caleb also saved those rock stars' careers. The lady had started losing her confidence which caused her much fear. Then Caleb had worked overtime, for which he got paid extra, which some would think is sublime. The rock stars couldn't get over you missing their concert so they gave you tickets for tomorrow with the signed guitar. This was way better than getting a new car, he would have to learn to play his guitar!

When you are feeling down and want to frown, ask yourself: *Are you only focusing on negative situations? Or are there other ways you can look for more positive interpretations?*

Why our brain will tango and dance with mental filtering

Mental filtering happens at the subconscious level; this is where people see something happen, and you ask them to tell you what happened. This explains why our stories are never the same. That's because these thinking villains once upon a time protected us. That was a different time— it was a different era.

Everyone wears virtual glasses to see the world. The glasses you choose to wear are mental filtering lenses. All information that comes in has to be processed through our mental filter, and if it weren't, we would suffer from an information overload. Mental filtering protects us from being overwhelmed.

Our brain receives over one million pieces of information every second delivered through our five senses. Ask yourself what you are choosing to focus on.

How to stop mental filtering villains by looking at the positive magnifier principle

Instead of seeing the glass half empty, take the opportunity to see the glass half full. First, take a deep breath and choose to magnify the positive instead of giving the negative more space to replicate.

Think of a picture of you outside playing in the rain. Now you decide to show this to your pal. Either your friend will look down and see the picture and comment that the rain is making everything wet or instead notice and comment upon you having fun playing.

Align with your values principle

What are the three top values in your life? Why do you wake up every morning and look forward to the day? Consider values to be your mental filtering guard, and that when you evaluate information, you make decisions around a hierarchy of your personal values.

If you value eating foods that will make you feel good, then your personal value of staying healthy will be filtered as you make choices at a restaurant ordering a meal from a menu.

Sometimes, it's easy to let mental filtering take over and become overwhelmed by so many food choices.

We may face the same dilemma when reading food labels: how do we ascribe value to certain ingredients in foods based on our personal knowledge, preferences and available information? In your daily life, identify your three top values. Write these down. Next to each value define what each one means to you, and give each one a rating from 1 to 10, with ten being very close to making choices based on your preferred value, and one being the least aligned to your personal values.

Finally, ask yourself, *what is one thing you can do or do differently to get to one number higher than where you are located now?* Consider this example with Caleb:

> "I listened to my gut and selected values which connected with me the most."

Value/Describe/Scale/Change
1. Family—it's measured by spending quality time with the people who matter the most and his current rating is 4/10. In order to achieve an increase to 5/10 every Friday, he will schedule a game night with his cousin on telehealth since everyone lives so far.

2. Exercise—measured by how much he moves his body every day for at least one hour as well as staying flexible. Current rating is 9/10. In order to achieve an increase to 10/10, Caleb must also walk for two hours each day around the park. He will also start stretching every morning for ten minutes to remain flexible.

3. Music—measured by how much he plays or listens to music each day to relax. Current rating is 1/10. In order to increase his score to 2/10, Caleb will buy a flute from a secondhand store and learn how to play after watching videos on YouTube.

Now, every morning after you wake up, consider your existing values and make any necessary adjustments to improve your outcome. And remember, it doesn't matter which value you choose; it's more important to be sincere and authentic to yourself and your established core values.

Core values list

Below is a list of core values commonly used by leadership institutes and programs. This list is not exhaustive, but it will give you an idea of some common core values (also called personal values). My recommendation is to select less than five core values to focus on—if everything is a core value, then nothing is really a priority.

Authenticity	Citizenship	Service
Achievement	Community	Spirituality
Adventure	Competency	Stability
Authority	Contribution	Success
Autonomy	Creativity	Status
Balance	Curiosity	Trustworthiness
Beauty	Determination	Wealth
Boldness	Fairness	Wisdom
Compassion	Optimism	Security
Challenge	Peace	Self-Respect

Bonus: Questions to better understand your values and take action instead of reaction

- Describe what each value means to you?
- Think about why this value is important to you?
- How is this value showing up in your life now?
- How might you behave if this value was not being validated by others?
- What positive changes might you see today to be more in keeping with your values?
- What could you start doing today to live more aligned with your values?

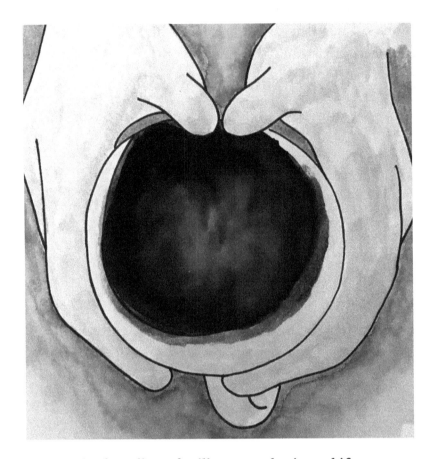

Think of a gallon of milk as your brain and if you were to drop one thought (represented by a drop of black food coloring ink) into the milk metaphor, it would completely change the milk's color (your brain matter) from white to pale gray. This analogy is one way of explaining what mental filtering does. Mental filtering takes, at face value, one bad, exclusive, dwelling thought and continues to repeat it in your brain until the whole milk solution or your personal situation turns completely black.

Cognitive triangle tool

You can use the cognitive triangle (shown in the image below) to show how thoughts, feelings, and behaviors can change the situations around you.

This model and imagery technique can help you to feel better and prevent worry and sadness.

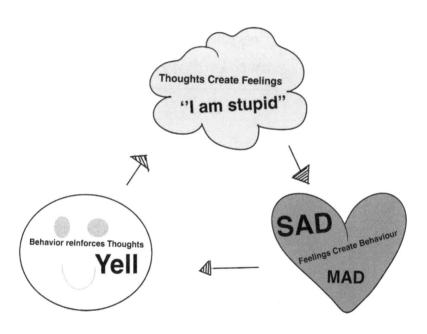

"Between stimulus and response there is a space. In that space is our power to choose our response. In our response lies our growth and our freedom."

~ VIKTOR E. FRANKL

Jumping to Conclusions, Mind Reading and Fortune Telling

My friend Rabbit

My friend Rabbit has this little nasty habit.
He loves to jump.
I am not talking about bouncing, boing and
    kurplump.
I am talking about jumping to conclusions.

This is where you are partially listening, and come up with your own solutions. For example, when Rabbit was talking to Sloth, Sloth turned completely red. Rabbit thought Sloth was getting mad, when really Sloth was sucking on a sour warhead.

That light hearted conversation.
Ended up causing a big miscommunication.
Rabbit yelled and stormed off, while
    Sloth was left in
    seclusion.
Rabbit cried in his
    own confusion.
That night he had a
    friend visit—little,
    yellow Canary.
She talked with
    Rabbit and said his
    actions had been
    arbitrary.

The next day when Rabbit went to
  apologize.
He got an unhappy surprise.
Sloth was looking like such a loner.
Hunched over looking sad in the corner.
Rabbit said, "Hello," and wondered why
  Sloth had gotten mad.

Sloth looked up and said, "I am sad.
  Yesterday, I thought I lost my best friend
  and comrade.
"You left without saying a word, I felt
  perturbed.
"And I didn't even know what had
  happened or occurred."
"Yeah, I know we were talking when your
  face got all red," Rabbit replied.

"I get the idea that you were getting mad at
me, but it was all in my head."

I am going to start making better choices. I will ask
others what they mean, before listening to those negative,
unhelpful voices. So when you find yourself thinking,
Wow, someone is being really mean, and get those mixed,
confusing feelings; remember to ask what's up. We never
know how others are dealing with their own wounds and
healings.

Why our brain will hopscotch and jump to conclusions

Jumping to a conclusion can be very helpful if a bear is chasing you so you can run. However, if a bear is not chasing you, then running around with these villains can only get you down. Jumping to a conclusion is when one makes an assumption about what someone else is going to say or do. Often, you will see people jumping to conclusions when saying certain words and phrases like "I know what you're going to say."

Sometimes, we can have a bad time at a party for example and think that we will continue to have a bad time at parties. This is known as believing you can predict the future, fortune telling, or forecasting. Another type of this fallacy is when you believe you know what someone else is thinking, which is called mind reading. We all have been guilty of it from time to time. Have you ever assumed you knew what your mother was thinking and ended up being wrong? When you think that she is not smiling at you because she is upset (and later realizing she just has a headache) is forecasting. When we do it more often than not, then maybe it's time to use our handy principles.

How to stop our brain from hopscotching with assorted villains principle

Put your thoughts on trial principle

Here are the steps

First, stick with the facts by identifying the situation. For example, I am lost at a concert and don't have my phone to call my parents.

Identify the moods

- Describe any emotions that come up associated with the situation, including positive and negative ones. For example, feeling scared.

Identify automatic thoughts

- List all the thoughts that come to mind when remembering the situation. Identify the thought that is most strongly a cognitive distortion or thinking villain. For example, I am never going to find my friends and will probably end up grounded for life.

Gather evidence

- Identify evidence that supports the irrational thought and identify evidence that does not support the thought. For example, I am never safe and will end up getting kidnapped.

Next, put each thought on trial one at a time

- Evidence Supporting Thought: "I am never safe."
- Evidence Not Supporting Thought: "I am never safe."

Find a balanced thought

- Finally, identify an alternative, more balanced and realistic appraisal about your situation. You can assume the role of judge and use evidence from both sides listed above to reach your final unbiased verdict. For example, I can ask for help from any police officer at the concert and I will not be lost. I am just scared and thinking the worst. Let me talk to the police now so I can get home.

Test your ability to see the whole picture principle

Typically distortions only let us see part of a picture, only one piece at a time. For example, when you see the hand of a person prior to seeing the rest of the arm. Try guessing what the entire picture represents.

Rubin's vase—also referred to as "The Two Face, One Vase Illusion" depicts the silhouette of a vase in black against a white background—along with the profiles of two inward-looking faces in white.

Test your skills

Which sentence represents jumping to conclusion (JC), mind reading (MR) or fortune telling (FT).

1. I had a horrible meal at the restaurant, I should not go back, it will always be gross.
2. I am not going to play with her because she is not looking at me when she is talking, and I know it means that she is not interested.
3. I do not think you lost your money, it probably was stolen.
4. I had fun at the school dance. I will always have fun at the school dance.

Answers: 1. FT, 2. MR, 3. JC, 4. FT

Emotion word search puzzle

S	F	E	A	R	F	U	L	Q
I	U	X	N	A	C	O	O	L
L	N	C	G	G	B	X	N	F
L	O	I	E	E	S	V	E	A
Y	D	T	R	S	E	O	L	K
B	U	E	T	A	S	N	Y	E
M	A	D	I	S	G	U	S	T
F	W	G	P	S	H	Y	A	S
B	C	M	T	Y	I	E	D	E
B	P	M	T	Y	Y	A	T	H

Emotions

Anger	Lonely	Fake	Fun
Cool	Mad	Fearful	Sassy
Disgust	Rage	Shy	Silly
Excited	Sad		

"You are not your illness. You have an individual story to tell. You have a name, a history, a personality. Staying yourself is part of the battle."

~ JULIAN SEIFTER

Chapter 5

Personalization

Scarlet

Scarlet is a beautiful hanging vine plant. In actuality though, she is not very confident. She is able to grow and climb walls, fences and trees. She loves hanging out with the humming birds and bees. Scarlet enjoys spreading and growing far and wide. She can take up space to the point that the other plants would often stop growing or collide. She would take up more space than others liked. Her plant friends were not very psyched.

One day, Scarlet came down with a cold. Her vines began to shrivel and fold. Not long after this, the other plants blossomed and grew. The bougainvillea finally blossomed flowers which were long overdue. Rose talked to Scarlet, hoping she would feel better soon, but then went on to show Scarlet how she had actually grown new petals that were pink.

Well, Scarlet started to think. "Rose likes me better when I shrink!" Scarlet's sour mood filled her with turmoil as her flowers drooped and vines continued to recoil. The hummingbirds visited her less often. She was very upset and called them out, without caution. The birds knew that since she was sick, they hoped that she would get better soon, but they wanted to try the other sweet pollen they didn't get to try as often. Scarlet wished she had a witty comeback or ended that conversation throwing a punch. Her stomach hurt and she was light-headed, but she had no appetite and skipped lunch. Her heart was racing, and the place she loved to call home felt much less welcoming or embracing.

Everyone in the garden told Scarlet to get better soon. But they then showed each other how they never looked this good in mid-June! All the while, Scarlet continued to shrink, droop, dwindle, and wilt. She asked herself, had she really been that conceited as she filled her mind with negative feelings of guilt. Her friend, Violet, came up to her one day and asked her if she was feeling okay. "You seem well, but I see you continue to dwell. Do you continue to feel ill, or do you have a chill?"

Scarlet told Violet that she was physically fine, and she hasn't been trying to whine. She had just been feeling like everyone hates her due to thriving so well, as she has shriveled up and things are not like they were. Violet replied, "All the plants, flowers and trees are very happy to be thriving, but they have no ill will and want you to do more than just surviving."

Violet then went on to talk about how everyone in the garden could practice being more mindful through their interactions. Mindfulness is where one is thinking about others' feelings with respect, empathy and being thoughtful in their actions.

Scarlet started to grow after that day. A new ladder was added to the garden so that all the flowers could be on full display. Scarlet unraveled and grew and the whole garden was starting to look brand new. Scarlet learned that just because people are proud of who they are, this doesn't mean you can't be just as magnificent for being the star that you are.

Why the brain will use magic mirrors with the personalization villains principle

Blame or personalization is how we protect our ego at times. If you blame others then usually you will not be the one to take the fall. Personalization is when we take that blame and turn it around towards ourselves. We lose our own power when we blame others. Think about it. Here are some useful examples of personalization:

- Thinking that things are your fault, if someone else doesn't have a good time when they are spending time with you.

- Feeling like you are being left out with your friends when you see your buddies are leaving you out.

Stop negative self-talk principle

It can sometimes be nice to listen to your own inner voice, but once this inner voice becomes an annoying, negative, repeating record player then it's time to stop the negative self-talk. You can do this simply by visualizing a BIG, RED, STOP SIGN and begin to talk the walk. Here are some examples:

Negative self-talk	Positive thinking
I'm too lazy to get this done.	I wasn't able to fit it into my schedule, priorities.
There's no way it will work.	I can try to make it work.
I don't want to do anything	I prefer to sit here and rest

Self-talk activity

Which statement takes accountability rather than placing blame:

I am late to class and I'm not sure what happened. My mom was supposed to wake me up for school.

or

I am late to class so I will set an alarm to prevent this happening in the future.

I think we should try harder to be happy together.

or

I will try harder to be happy.

The team performed terribly, and it was a waste of my time.

or

I will try harder in the future, and this was helpful to learn.

Drop the perfect person act principle

Catch your critic being perfect. The goal here is progress not perfection. No one is perfect and can never be. Perfection is an illusion, a magic trick. When you give up trying to be perfect, you start a chance of getting to know who you are and recognize that perfection becomes an imperfect (and often unattainable) stressful destination.

Check your responsibility principle

When you are taking full responsibility for a situation ask yourself: *am I responsible for the way they feel or think?*

Check your Control Principle

When you feel yourself taking things personally during a situation, ask yourself *what* you are actually in control of currently. Next, ask yourself, . . . *am I in control over what I am blaming myself for in this situation?*

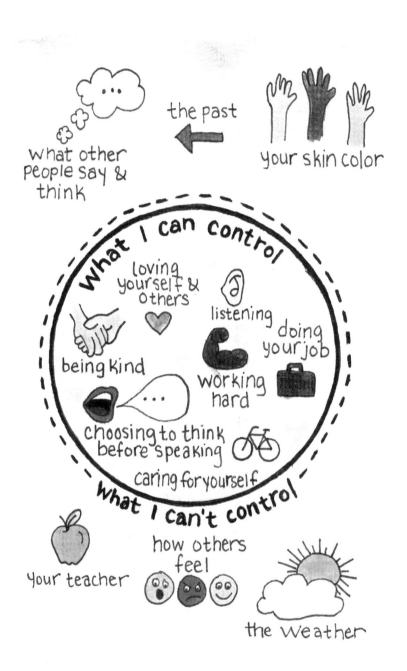

Stop telling the story principle

When we tell our stories to others, it's usually because we want to be heard. This can be helpful to feel better at times, however, when we are recounting our stories to others, it can be tempting to add a little more flavor to our story than needed. We can then catch ourselves blaming others for things which they had no possible control over to begin with. Next time you are telling your story of events to another person, consider your own motivations in telling the story. You need to ask yourself: *what is my reason for telling this story? Is it to empower others or to take away their power?*

"Watch your thoughts, they become words; watch your words, they become actions; watch your actions, they become habits; watch your habits, they become character; watch your character, for it becomes your destiny."

~ FRANK OUTLAW

Chapter

6

···

Emotional Reasoning

···

Angel

Angel was a very peculiar *mademoiselle.* She was shy and it took her a while to come out of her shell. Everything needed to be a certain way. She lived a modest life and felt normal and certainly nothing spectacular. Angel was walking home late one night when she was startled by a furious monster; it gave her quite a fright.

When she told her friends the story, they all thought she was very courageous. Little did she know, her fight or flight status started stimulating the big nerve that runs from one's head to one's gut, called the vagus. From that night on, she became very emotional and her thoughts were irrational. She pretended to be okay as her emotions walked a fine line.

The next day, she was going berry picking with a friend but ended up being pricked by a thorn. Her shirt was torn and the rest of the day she yelled, "This is a horrible day." She yelled and yelled as loud as a car horn.

Well, her friends did not want to hang out with someone who yelled in their face so they left without a trace; this gave Angel some much needed time and space. This did not help her as she cried and sat on the side of the curb. Why did she feel so disturbed?

She went and got a delicious coffee and felt much better while eating some caramel toffee. *Perfect,* she thought, *the rest of the day is going to be okay.* She set off for work to get some papers filed. During all this time, she laughed with coworkers and smiled. Her friends met up with her the next day and asked if she was doing okay. Angel was surprised and claimed she felt good. Her friends did not seem to understand, but they did the best they could. Yesterday, you seemed pretty upset and didn't respond, but reacted. Her friends stated they felt attacked and did not like the vibes or energy Angel had extracted.

Angel was lost and confused, she didn't remember her day going that way. She remembered feeling warm and happy drinking her latte. She stated, "I didn't like picking berries, that's for sure."

"Ever since I ran into that monster, I have been overwhelmed in ways that are obscure. After work, I tend to feel like I'm watching my life, instead of living life."

"I am walking home late at night, on edge—hyper-aware my senses are sharp as a knife. I am very scared, and emotionally impaired."

One of Angel's friends spoke, "That monster you saw gave you quite the scare; your brain knows you're okay, but your fight or flight system is still frightened; it was more than it could bear."

Your body needs to heal from the frightening trauma, for you could have been badly hurt; it's the same feeling you get when you're excited after going to a great concert. What I am trying to say is that it's totally normal if you're feeling a little neurotic; unfortunately, there is no medicine for this momentary illness or an antibiotic.

Remember, our feelings can lie, just because we feel scared even with no present danger, our mind takes us back when we think we might die. Start living in the present moment and do not postpone it. While talking kindly to our body, there is no need to make an atonement.

Why the brain will weaken when using emotional reasoning

When we feel things, it feels so real. We can easily believe that since we feel something then that proves that it is real. Wrong! Emotions have a purpose. Emotions tell us what's going right and what needs to be worked on.

Emotions are not facts; emotions are only energy that can have any skin you please, cheese. You can be both scared or excited about your first day at school or camp. Being both scared and excited are things that people can choose to feel on their first day.

Which one will you choose to feel on your first day? Will you choose to be scared or excited? You feel something but the feelings could be a response from something that happened years ago. And you can end up treating a current situation or person unfairly because of your remembered past experiences.

For example, you might be walking down the street and think, *I feel anxious so I know something dangerous is going to happen;* or *I feel so depressed, this must be the worst place to go to school.*

How to stop the emotional reasoning villains principles

The "I feel therefore it is not" principle

If you don't have any firm evidence other than simply relying upon the way you feel, then this is not enough evidence to say whether something is true or not. Doubting yourself is normal. Letting it stop you is a choice. If you feel it, wait before you believe until you have all evidence. Remember no one **MAKES** you angry. You **DECIDE** to use anger as a response.

The "what boundaries are and feel like" principle

- It's not my job to fix others.

- It's okay if others get angry.

- It's okay to say no.

- It's not my job to take responsibilities for others.

- I don't have to anticipate the needs for others.

- It's my job to make me happy.

- Nobody has to agree with me.

- I have the right to set and have limits and space.

- I am enough.

Boundary activity

Find and circle the Goldilocks Boundary

You don't want your boundary to be too hard, or too soft. You want your boundaries to be just right so you can feel balance.

1) **A.** I'll tell others everything about me.

   B. I like to share information about myself that's relevant to the conversation.

   C. I rather not share at all.

2) **A.** I love hugs, so I will hug everyone.

   B. I love hugs, but I will not ask others if they would like a hug.

   C. I love hugs and I will ask before I hug others.

The "what self-care can look like" principle

When people say you need some self-care, here are some ideas that might be helpful . . .

Emotional	Physical	Social
• Journaling • Writing songs/ Stories • Reflecting on your emotions	• Sports • Working out • Getting enough sleep • Eating nutritional foods • Hot bubble baths • Taking walks with your dog or out in nature	• Phone call to a friend • Attending social events with people you care about • Talking less with people who bring you down. • Laughing

Spiritual	Mental	Do What You Love
• Meditation • Prayer • Practicing gratitude • Being outside in nature and using all five senses • Listening to music	• Puzzles • Reading • Playing a musical instrument • Learning a new language • Learning something new	

The "ride the wave" principle

First experience your emotion
As a wave coming and going
Don't try to get rid of emotions
Don't push it away
Don't block it or suppress it
Don't hold on to it
Just let is raise, peak and fall away
Just ride the wave

"Self-Discipline begins with the mastery of your thoughts. If you don't control what you think, you can't control what you do."

~ NAPOLEON HILL

7

Catastrophizing

Tamara

Tamara was very excited to go to the airport to pick up Grandma. Once a year, they planned a special week for just the two of them. Last year, they went to San Diego where they visited the many beaches and a world-famous zoo. Her grandma traveled to many places, seeing the cultures and people of all races. So this week, it was special to see grandma all on her own. Grandma was there for her and her alone.

Grandma was running late . . . Did she have the right date? Tamara double checked her cellphone, and wondered if she had a bad cell phone Wi-Fi zone. She was supposed to come by plane and not take the overnight train. Tamara told herself to breathe and not to frown; this was no time to have a meltdown. Her plane may have been delayed because of the rain, or possibly a hurricane! "No, no, no. I need to stop with these troubling thoughts." Her stomach felt all tied up in knots.

Grandma's phone may not be on or just unplugged, or worse, she got in a brawl and was slugged. How Tamara wished her grandma would just call. Grandma may just be caught up on a phone call. Did her health decay from high cholesterol? What if she did not show up—that would be the worst thing of all! Blown away in some tornadoes, lost in a storm in Barbados? Fallen in some random ditch, or hexed by some wicked witch. Suffering in poison ivy, needing to claw and scratch that really bad itch? Spooked to death by a ghost, poisoned by some bad toast, she didn't know what scared her the most! Stung by a bee, or lost at sea, maybe stuck up in a tree, well, that would be a sight to see!

Did grandma make her flight, or get stuck in a snowstorm and have frostbite? Maybe she got struck by lighting, oh, how that would be so frightening! Bitten by a dog, poisoned by a frog, sleeping off the eggnog—seriously, Tamara, stop with this negative dialogue!

It was quarter past two, whatever should she do? Seriously though, what could she do? The arrivals showed the plane had landed. Okay, so was Tamara being reprimanded? "Tamara, Tamara," someone was calling her name—or at least she thought she heard it. She was starting to feel quite lame. Grandma was standing behind her and smiled, "Sorry, I think I told you the wrong baggage claim . . ."

All of Tamara's thoughts seemed so absurd. Tamara and Grandma finally greeted and at once Tamara's worries were deleted. Tamara and Grandma were ready for their vacation, called a cab, and headed off towards their destination! Oh my, what a happy sensation!

My emotional hierarchy scale principle

Things I Enjoy	Rank	Things That Upset Me	Rank

In this activity you will need to write or draw out things that you enjoy or do not like. Then rank each activity. The point of this activity is to become aware of things that upset you and learn how you can best prepare for any given situation. You can use a scale of 1-10 to rank your emotions with 10 indicating the most negative response to your situation.

Remember there are no wrong emotions, it's how we act on those emotions that matter!

Why the brain is patronizing when using catastrophizing villains

When we engage with these catastrophizing villains, we tend to blow things out of proportion. This can mean thinking the worst will happen and believing irrational thoughts. People use catastrophic thinking patterns as a way of protecting themselves from getting hurt.

Think about a time when you thought I will just expect the worst, so if I don't get in the school play then I won't be upset. But now you understand your internal dialogue (essentially what you say to yourself) has the ability to manifest your current reality. In this way, catastrophizing can keep you in a repeating state of spiraling downwards.

The "are you spiraling" principle

1. **Igniting Event**
   Something that MUST or MUST NOT happen—
   instead just observe and be more curious.

2. **Judgment**
   Making conclusions—instead stay open.

3. **Core Beliefs**
   Assumptions based on conclusions—instead do
   not be so willing to accept.

4. **Response**
   Reaction to belief conclusion—instead of react,
   act.

5. **Reinforce**
   Supports and focuses on the negative talking—
   instead utilize positive self-talk.

6. **Restart** the cycle of catastrophizing.

7. **Spiral Down**
   Instead assumptions are not proof. Stay curious
   my friends.

Spiraling Activity

Circle which statement shows a person about to catastrophize:

1) **A.** The sky is dark and that means it's going to rain so I should take cover.

   B. I watched the news today and they said it was going to rain.

2) **A.** If I don't get into college, I will end up homeless.

   B. If I don't get into college, I could still work and rent a room.

Answers: 1. A, 2. A

The transmutation principle

Grapes must be crushed to make wine.
Diamonds form under pressure.
Olives are pressed to release oil.
Seeds grow in darkness.

Whenever you feel crushed, under pressure, pressed, or in the darkness, you are in a powerful place of transformation. Remember to allow yourself to ride the waves and let things pass.

Transmutation activity

Choose the matching word to the transmutation:

If you want to have	=	Then you need
Hard Work		Quit
Success		Bitterness
Happiness		Acceptance
Love		Gratitude
Hate		Consistency
Failure		Determination

Answers: hard work=determination, success=consistency, happiness=gratitude, hate=bitterness, failure=quit

The "keep a worry journal" principle

Get them out on paper and out of your head. Set a timer for three minutes and start writing as many worries as you can. Now, you will have to wait till the next day to allow yourself to worry again so you can write them down.

For your *Worry Time Journal,* schedule between three to five minutes each day to just write. This is a great way to express your feelings in a safe way and to return later to your writing and see if there are patterns emerging which are making you more prone to worry.

"Success is neither magical nor mysterious. Success is the natural consequence of consistently applying the basic fundamentals."

~ JIM ROHN

Chapter

8

Magical Thinking

Gabriel

Gabriel was in the fourth grade, he received B's and A's, played baseball and had amazing friends he would never trade. He got along with his sister who was a little wild, for a six-year-old child. His life was almost perfect, except that his parents often argued and called each other names in disrespect.

His parents often participated in yelling competitions and accused each other of their suspicions. They yelled, argued and blamed each other with different accusations. One night, during a particularly heated argument, his dad stormed off and was out, "bam," turned off like a flashlight.

Gabriel was very worried and knew something was not right. He thought to himself, if only I get straight A's, his parents would have better days. Tomorrow, he will look for his lucky number six, so his dad will come back and everything will be alright with one quick fix.

The next day when he and his sister went out to get ice cream, they only had one more scoop of his and his sister's favorite flavor. He gave it to her so there would be no misbehavior. Things were going smooth and on track, now his dad would come back.

When he got home, he cleaned his room, polished his shoes and even rearranged his baseball caps. Gabriel did his homework and helped his sister, so there were no chances for mishaps. During dinner, Gabriel ate

everything, even the lame green, boring vegetable. There would be no excuse for mom or dad to be miserable.

His daddy came back, but his mom looked displeased. Gabriel ran up to him and cried as they hugged and squeezed. His dad apologized and stated it is never okay to just storm off like he did, even when you're angry and upset. It was no excuse, but he loved Gabriel and his sister, and that they should never forget. His father was home and full of regret. His dad had returned and hoped his children could forgive him for his mistakes. After dinner, Gabriel's dad said he would take Gabriel and his sister out for milkshakes.

The next morning, his parents gathered the family together for some big news. His parents stated it was better for them to split, but there was no one to accuse. His parents stated they were getting a divorce, and it wasn't anyone's fault, of course.

Their marriage had ended and it was not what they had intended.

"We know at times we have yelled as loud as a thunderbolt, but it was never anyone's fault. We understand our behavior has been mysterious, only because we knew our choices were serious. It had nothing to do with you both being curious. Just because mom's and dad's feelings have changed doesn't mean we don't love you the same!" We couldn't ask for greater kids they both said without shame.

Gabriel now has two homes and splits time with his parents, but he knows his sister and himself are not to blame.

Why the brain is tricked when using magical thinking villains

Magical thinking is a way the brain is able to remove unwanted thoughts through ritual thinking. Rituals can be problematic, painful, and timely. For example, if you believe that if you wash your hands six times in a row, you will have better sleep. This ritual may work but you may still wake up with irritated red hands from overwashing.

Some people use magical thinking for motivation and believe that it will allow them to win. Have you ever put on your lucky shirt so you could win your game, maybe knocked on some wood to keep misfortune away, or how about making a wish blowing on a dandelion? Or how about believing bad things come in threes, or you will have seven years of bad luck for breaking a mirror?

Exposure principle

Confront your fears instead of using magical thinking. It may be hard to play your game without your lucky shirt, but you should play anyway and focus on having fun in the moment. Eventually, you'll get used to playing in a different shirt and make new memories associated with winning.

Response principle

To reverse magical thinking, you have to resist ritual behavior and undo your do.

Exposure and Response Activity

Scenario 1: Imagine you are afraid of germs. If you wanted to practice exposure and response would you:

    (a)   Brush against the toilet and resist washing your hands?

    (b)   Brush against the toilet and wash your hands four times with warm water?

Scenario 2: You have a school presentation and you are afraid to speak in front of crowds, would you:

(a) Not show up for class and instead drop out?

(b) Show up and do the best you can, using suggested steps to help you speak in front of groups of people without feeling afraid?

Restructuring worries principle

First, ask yourself, what are you worried about? Next, how likely is it that your worries will come true? Give examples of past experience. Now, ask yourself if your worries do come true, what's the worst that could happen? Next, ask yourself if your worries come true, what's most likely going to happen? Lastly, ask yourself if your worries come true, what are the chances you'll be okay. . . .

In one week? 0-100% In one month? 0-100% In a year? 0-100%

"If 50 million believe in a fallacy,
it is still a fallacy."

~ PROF. SAMUEL WARREN CAREY

Chapter 9

Control Fallacies—External and Internal

Veronica

Veronica was a really lucky primate who had everything she ever wanted from her many fabulous dates. You could say Veronica would be considered a privileged orangutan today. Veronica lived in a forest with tons of palm trees in the lush, moist, green forests high in the mountains, the trees draped with vines and soft mosses. Her home was stylish and sat inside one of the tallest trees standing in the Forest of Fallacies known for reasoning that is logically incorrect.

Veronica is sacred and would sit with her legs crossed and her arms by her side all day and night without ever leaving her spot. The law in the forest said that Veronica was sitting in the sacred spot. Veronica, at the age of three, lost her mother and father to a poaching accident due to deforestation because of the production of palm oil and wrong beliefs.

Veronica was mute and blind from the accident, and since her parents did not survive, she became the next ruler in line as royalty in the Forest of Fallacies. Veronica used hasty generalization fallacies and concluded that since humans burned her home down, all men were forest burners.

Veronica and all the animals believed that Veronica controlled all of the animals' thoughts and beliefs and ran the forest with her mind as she pleased. Even the birds sang songs while in the forest, praising Veronica and saying that she was the reason that the sun would rise each morning. Even the Koalas would never worry about their drinking water since Veronica's presence would make the skies drizzle away every single day and fresh cold water rivers made their way.

All the animals in the Forest Of Fallacies knew Veronica was in control of all their possibilities known as the "cum hoc ergo propter hoc" fallacy. Each forest animal believed as long as Veronica remained the Queen Of Fallacies, everyone would be safe and sound from all that is not good. The animals came to believe that Veronica was responsible for their happiness inside the forest.

One day, Veronica sounded her thundering horn which was heard throughout the land. She announced a meeting, telling animals of the forest, both big and small, that a new law called the *Fallacies of Fairness* is being put into place. Veronica told the animals that she received a vision from the elders in her dream that the forest was now under a new law that would start at the first stroke of the moonlight hour and that everyone thereafter would start to make the same amount of food for their work in the forest regardless of who they were.

In the past, there had been many complaints about the lack of fairness in the forest where some animals, such as the tigers, received more food than the smaller animals. Or the stronger elephants, who eat more grass than the sloths. Veronica's message was that everyone will work, and each one will receive the same amount no matter who you may be, strong or weak, big or small.

Miron, the oldest Tiger in the forest spoke up and said:

"This is ridiculous and not fair. We are faster and we deserve more food, even if we only hunt for twenty minutes a day and the mongoose can take all day."

Then another louder voice spoke up; it was Rav, the elephant, who shouted that he did not agree with the new law and even considered it to be unfair. Rav thought that the elephants should continue to entertain the straw man fallacies and have more food since elephants were stronger than the rest of the crew.

Soon after, one of the smaller forest omnivores, Milles, the badger, stood up and asked Veronica:

> "Why do you think that Miron and Rav think that it is okay for them to work a little and rest all day while we work from sunrise until Sunday?"

Milles then said, "I think I may have a good idea; why don't we have a gathering, a hunt to see who can collect the most nuts after one full day? If we win, then the law of fairness will stay, and we will continue to share blessings and have the same amount of food for everyone—not based on the amount of work produced."

All the large animals like the panthers and giant pandas began to chuckle and laugh. They said: "How, since you are so small in stature, do you think that you're going to collect and produce more than all of us?"

One thing that Milles kept to himself was that winter was coming any day, and he knew that the weather could be what might just help the smaller animals win the hunt.

Rav turned to Veronica and said, "You are the Queen and we are grateful that you have always made everything right for us." Milles interrupted Rav and said:

"We have all been mistaken. Veronica, our Queen, is not the reason the sun shines each morning or that we have food on trees. We have all been deceived. This Is a circuit fallacy."

Milles then said:

"I have gone to the other side of the mountain and have seen other animal tribes in the forest and they have no queen. They also have the warm sun and abundance of food without any fallacies."

Miron spoke up and said:

"Maybe Milles is right. Our forest burned down because of man's ignorance, and after taking our trees, they left. Everything grew back because of time, not because of anything else."

No one seemed to believe Milles, not even the smaller animals. Even a few of the others thought that this was maybe a trap from Milles to get Veronica out of her treehouse where she would lose her ability to keep the world spinning.

A few of the other elephants were getting ready for a nap and wanted to get the hunt over with. One said, "This should take no time. After all, look at us and look at them."

The hunt had begun and all the larger animals decided to each gather nuts for fifteen minutes and store them together near the scale. Nothing else had to be done until the morning. After less than an hour, all the large animals had collected their nuts, stored them, and went to bed. So they would be ready to laugh at all the smaller animals because of their greater productivity.

Meanwhile, the smaller animals were nervous and did not understand why Milles would have set them up for failure. Milles told them, "Guys, don't worry, I have a plan."

Milles reminded the rest that no test was too big for them because Veronica was never the reason why things would work out. The truth is that everything works together, and when we come together, we can move mountains—no matter how big or small we may be.

Milles told all the animals a story he had overheard at the bottom of the mountain where he was never supposed to be because of the danger posed by the

humans. The story that Milles told was about the rabbit and the turtle. Milles said the rabbit ridicules the turtle for being slow and challenges the turtle to a race. In the race, the rabbit soon leaves the turtle behind and being confident of winning, decides to stop for a nap midway in the race. Upon awakening, the rabbit finds that his competitor (the turtle) was crawling slowly ahead and

won the race—arriving at the finish line before him.

All the animals were wondering how this story applied to them. Their challenge was how to get the most nuts rather than a race to the finish line. Milles continued by saying:

> "Tonight, all we need to do is climb up the mountain. I know it will be hard and challenging, but when the sun rests in the west, and the wind starts to blow, all the nuts will begin to fall down; we just need

to think of a way to get them to fall down here. That's where I was hoping Beavers would come in. If we cut the tree down with beaver teeth, the tree will fall and the winter wind will blow all the tree nuts down to us."

The animals responded:

"What a great idea. If you are right, Milles (said one of the beavers), then that would prove that Veronica is not the reason life continues on for some and not for all."

Milles then went on to say that he had heard the humans talk about this, and that this is why our forest is called the Forest of Fallacies. They say humans will bring other humans here to mislead them.

This is why Veronica does not know or understand what is happening to her because she **Assumes** something and never **Challenges** or looks at the evidence instead of her feelings for the truth.

The animals said: "We don't have much time."

One of the squirrels screamed out, "Let's get going!"

All the small animals climbed up the mountain. All of the animals, not just the beavers, started to saw down the tree with their teeth. The north wind blew and blew and by the time the tree fell down, hundreds and thousands of nuts came rolling down the mountain.

At last, the sun came up. Not only did the small animals beat the big animals by ten fold, Veronica believes that the curse on her was removed and her sight came back as now she saw the truth.

Now, the tiger and the elephants were not happy and had no clear basis for their arguments. However, Milles told them that before you were more than ready to eat all the food because you thought that fairness was about who was faster or stronger. The next time you are proving your point, take a few seconds and look for exaggeration and attacks.

Why the brain becomes misled by using fallacies villains

When we believe something because of our deeply-held beliefs and core values, this can color our perception of reality. This can create a Fallacy Villain—a false belief which can trick our brains into believing something which isn't true.

For example, most of the time we assume that our response is the correct response without really thinking about what the other person has gone through. Have you ever thought, well if a person loves me then they will do this thing for me. And if they don't, then that means they mustn't really love me. Someone can easily think this way if their experiences in their life are based on what others are prepared to do for them.

Some children growing up receive constant praise for their hard work, but when they grow up, they find that their bosses don't praise them as much. In this way, they don't feel as if they are worthy or good enough. This is a fallacy of belief.

The "stick to our guns" principle

If you have a hard time with being wrong, and you will stick to your guns at all costs then you are choosing to struggle with fallacies. Being wrong can be difficult, especially when it is around parents or peers, but it's important to allow yourself to make mistakes so you can grow.

So start by giving yourself permission to make mistakes. Next, open your mind and let yourself become curious about other people's opinions by asking more questions.

And take what you've heard to rethink your argument before you defend it and throw out your guns.

The "don't be critical of the critic" principle

It's okay to have your own opinion and others can have theirs, too. Sometimes, people feel scared when others may think differently than they do. We don't have to have others feel and think the same way as us to be okay. We do not have to compromise our values to be accepted by others. When someone may think differently from us or feel critical, it's okay, just let them be them.

Logical fallacies—some common examples

An **ad hominem fallacy** is an attack against an opponent's character rather than an attack against an argument or idea. For example, you might think:

> We should not play with the new girl since she cheated on a test when she was younger.

The **hasty generalization** fallacy is when a claim draws a conclusion based upon insufficient evidence. This can be seen in the following statement:

> "All women are bad drivers."

The straw man argument is when you attack your opponent's weakest argument rather than focusing upon their strongest. Consider the following example of this:

> "The governor says that we shouldn't fund the afterschool program for low income people. I disagree entirely. I can't understand why he wants to leave us defenseless like that."

Activity—Identify the Fallacy

1. Kelly is running for class president. In her campaign speech she says, "My opponent does not deserve to win. She is a liar and she cheated on her best friend last year." What fallacy has Kelly committed?

    a. Ad hominem
    b. Hasty generalization
    c. Straw man

2. Jack is preparing to create a commercial for a new energy drink. He visits a local college and surveys students in a math class about their beverage preferences. The majority of the class says they prefer apple-flavored drinks so Jack tells his superiors that apple is the flavor favored most by college students. What error in reasoning has Jack made?

    a. Ad hominem
    b. Hasty generalization
    c. Straw man

3. Consider the following exchange: Don: I think capital punishment is a necessary component of our justice system and should remain legal. Other: So you are saying that murder should be legal and it is okay for us to go around killing people just because we think they deserve it? That isn't right. Which type of fallacy is Don guilty of?

   a. Ad hominem
   b. Hasty generalization
   c. Straw man

Ad hominem

Ad hominem means "to the man" in Latin. People who use this fallacy typically attack a person directly rather than actually refuting that person's arguments. Louise's opponent's infidelity and smoking habit have no bearing on her ability to be class president.

Straw man

Straw man is a fallacy whereby a person builds up an exaggerated "straw man" version of the original argument and then attacks that version. Don has an easier time arguing against the idea that he endorses murder than he would attacking his original argument.

Hasty generalization

A hasty generalization is when someone assumes that what is true for a few people is true for all people. Just because one class likes apple drinks, it does not mean that all college students will.

*"Birds born in a cage think flying
is an illness."*

~ ALEJANDRO JODOROWSKY

Chapter 10

Disqualifying the Positive

Regan

Regan was younger than her sister and brother, Tegan and Keagan. Tegan was known for her artistic abilities in the arts. While Keagan was known for being academically smart, Regan didn't know what she was good at or what was her part. She tried playing a sport, only to find out that volleyball is very challenging if you are short. She could hardly serve the ball mid-court!

Regan thought maybe running in a race would be more her pace. She was fast, but only got third place. She wanted to win first place if she was going to be sweating and have a red face. Regan thought, *I am not good at anything! Maybe I will try to sing.* Regan tried out for the school choir. She made it, but it wasn't the part she had desired prior.

Regan joined the chess team, she realized quickly that the players were quite extreme. Being on a chess team was not what the TV shows made it seem! Poor Regan, she was never going to be as creative as Teagan or as smart as Keagan. She could run, but it wasn't fun.

Her sister and brother didn't seem to have to put in much work and Regan started to feel like a jerk. Regan just wanted to stop, quit, and give up since she made herself believe that she was just not enough.

As soon as Regan was ready to throw in the towel, her father ran in and asked his youngest: "Why The frown?"

Regan told her dad, "Well, it's just that everything I do

is wrong, it seems like, and I am never going to be great at anything."

That's when Regan's father said:

> "That's not what I noticed. See Regan, when you were playing volleyball, the team won because of your height, that's right! The ball was able to fly above your head, and so your teammates had a better advantage."

"You won third place and that's one more than your friend, North, who won the 4th. Regan, you may have not liked the royal game of chess, but after playing, now you appreciate playing checkers so much more when you play with your sister and have the highest score. Or how about when you tried out for choir, and after watching the band play, you were curious and

started inquiring about different instruments? Soon after, you were downloading apps to learn to play cymbals and drums."

"Oh, my dear Regan, do you not see how much you are seeing the worst in everything you do, instead of not seeing your best? Start by positive self-talk and all that starts with you."

Why the brain becomes biased when using disqualifying the positive villains

People will use "Disqualifying the Positive" thinking villains when we experience something that is good, or even neutral, and we convince ourselves that it is not actually positive. We find ways to reject these experiences, insisting that they don't matter or count.

Examine your personal biases principle

Why do you hold them?
Are they justified by the evidence?
Do you want them to be true?
Are you afraid they might be true?
Did you just make them up?

Feelings are not facts principle

When you're feeling down or stressed, would you say your thoughts are mostly positive or negative? If you're like most people, negative thoughts run wild and you might feel that you have trouble controlling them and that changes your feelings into facts.

Make a list of your positive attributes and accomplishments. Try to accept compliments when people give them to you with a simple "thank you."

Ask yourself:

- If that doesn't count, what does count?

- Who decides what counts and what doesn't?

- Why do you think good things can't happen to you?

Shoulds and absolutes test

Out of the statements below, can you guess which ones would be considered a cognitive distortion?

1. I never want to pick up my room!

2. When my grandmother comes to stay with us, I sometimes clean my room because I know she appreciates it.

3. Before I got a dog, I never knew why people liked dressing their dog up in clothes.

4. I have never received a good grade in math!

5. You should always get 8 hours of sleep.

6. Fantasy books are the best!

7. Dogs always see in black and white.

8. When I am able to, I prefer to buy my coffee, rather than make it at home.

9. Friday the 13th is known for being an unlucky day.

10. Small dogs are always yappy.

Answers:

1. No. 1 is considered a cognitive distortion because this person may want to clean up their room. A more appropriate statement would be "Most days, I don't clean my room, or I don't mind when my room is a little messy."

2. This is not considered a cognitive distortion because this person most likely cleans up her room at times when her grandmother visits. You can't argue with this statement.

3. This statement isn't a cognitive distortion because this person previously failed to understand why people dressed up their pets, but now has a different point of view since owning one.

4. This statement is tricky, one because people have subjective opinions of what a good grade is. Some people may need an A and others are fine with passing grades. So this is a cognitive distortion.

5. This is a cognitive distortion because some people can function just fine with six or seven hours of sleep each night.

6. This one is a cognitive distortion because not all people think fantasy books are the best.

7. This is another cognitive distortion because not all dogs are able to see.

8. This one isn't a cognitive distortion because it's difficult to prove that this person always prefers to buy coffee. She qualifies her statement with the words, "when I am able to," which isn't all the time.

9. This one isn't a cognitive distortion because even if you don't believe Friday the 13th is unlucky, there are many people who believe that it is or have superstitions about it.

10. This one is a cognitive distortion. You may know more yappy little dogs, but other people can argue that their small dog, whatever a small dog looks like to them, is not yappy.

How did you do? Did any of these common statements surprise you?

Shoulds and Absolutes

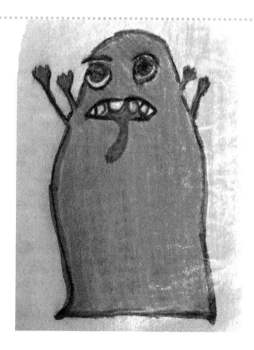

A story in spring

It was spring and, oh, how much joy it brings. It's when the baby birds learn to fly and challenge each other to see who's the fastest and how high each can fly. Most birds tried to avoid challenging the bald eagle because their family flew so majestically that they looked regal. Everyone thought Eagle should be disqualified from the challenge, or it should be illegal. The bald eagle family flew with such grace, such ease, but they never actually flaunted it.

Eagle's major competitor was Hawk. Hawk was not one to be so humble, but everyone knew Hawk practiced around the clock to win against Eagle. Crow, another competitor, was known for his head games; and often quit in the middle of the competition or just did not show. At first, the birds were upset by all his talk and squawk, but then realized Crow enjoyed upsetting everyone and being known as the foe with no intention in competing in what he referred to as a silly show.

Seagull often participated. He would often complain throughout the day before, telling everyone he overate and his stomach hurt because he was too full.

Parakeet enjoyed participating, which everyone thought was cute and sweet. Owl never participated, because he patrolled all night making sure everyone could get rest and sleep tight. No one made fun of him since none of the birds could make a decision if something happened to Owl during the competition as to who would take over the night position.

No one ever asked or bothered Chicken to participate, for his father cried and yelled every morning. All the

birds thought Rooster must not be right in the head and it was concerning. Dove, Raven, Hummingbird and Peacock loved to participate. They loved the fun and had no hate.

Parrot showed up and had a million questions and suggestions about how the competition should go. Parrot was always gossiping and chatting as if she was always in the know. Flamingo was always looking petite and only stood on one leg—they figured it was better if he just didn't compete.

Lastly, Duck decided to sign up, hoping that this year might just bring him more luck.

Everyone was shocked when they saw Ostrich was going to try and participate! Everyone laughed and mocked him saying:

> "Watch, you will accidentally oversleep and show up late!"

> "Whenever there is some form of competition, or heated conversations, your family avoids it and puts their heads in the sand." You may tower over us and look all big and grand, but really you are too big to leave the comfortable grassland."

> "Come on, haven't you heard, you are the largest bird, you are not capable of flying, why are you trying? How can such a big bird fly, that is just absurd!"

> "You're overweight and have no chance of winning, why even start from the beginning?

Ostrich replied, "I understand. My family is known each year to not compete because they tend to have lots of fear. You just watch; I will enter this competition, I am not like my ancestors for I am filled with ambition!"

Well, on the day of the flying high competition, all competitors lined up in anticipation. It was quite the sight, you see. All these different birds in one place and many animals watching from the land, sea and trees. There were many bets going on. All bets had to be placed before dawn.

Eagle always won so bets placed on him were assured. The animals observing were setting up camp and getting ready, they tried to get the best view so they wouldn't miss a thing just to make sure!

Tucán was this year's sportscaster because Parrot was always too opinionated and it was a disaster!

> "Okay everyone, this year's competitors are Eagle, Hawk, Seagull, Peacock, Raven, Duck, Dove, Parrot, Parakeet, Hummingbird and Ostrich; yes, you heard me right! Ostrich— the anchored down bird, who sticks his head in the sand when in fright! Looks like this year we will have a few surprises and I am full of delight!"

"Rules of the game—no contact, that was part of the contract. Secondly, if once you start to lower or go slower but for your safety, you are out. Because you start to descend quickly, don't try and mess about! Those are the only rules so don't even try me, fools!"

Eagle and Hawk were up first and Hawk looked like he had a lot of anger that had been allowed to fester. Up they flew so high in the sky, then Hawk tried to kick Eagle; wow what a cheater! Disqualified, Hawk! The crowd was in shock.

Next flyers up were Raven and Seagull—for those betting this was a difficult pick. They took off with gusto; when the birds could hardly be seen, Seagull's stomach started to hurt and he got sick! He started to fall, quicker than a brick.

Eagle saved him, he was significantly quick! So far, Eagle and Raven move on; next up: Parrot and Duck! They flew much higher than expected and the crowd was awestruck. Then, just with Duck's luck, he started to lower. Parrot moves on after the round.

Three contenders are up next: Parakeet, Hummingbird and Dove. There was no messing around. Dove was the first to take off and be high and above. Parakeet was just behind, but insisted he had forgotten the rules because when he left the ground, he gave Hummingbird a big shove. Well, this was the farthest Hummingbird had ever reached in the competition so Dove pretended to fall; no one had made that prediction! Hummingbird moves on.

Now, the last two competitors, which we have all wanted to see with high demand. Let's give a warm welcome to Peacock and Ostrich as they take the stand. Everyone leaned in to mock, tweet, and squawk as they viewed. Ostrich's long neck hovered above, he was trying to do anything to intimidate and use his skills to make due. Peacock launched with one massive leap, only to crash into Ostrich and be disqualified from the heat.

Oh, Wow, that was cheap, and an embarrassing way to get beat! Tomorrow is the final day of the competition, the remaining birds are Ostrich, Eagle, Raven, Parrot, and Hummingbird. In the many years of this race taking place, this has never occurred. The crowd was dead silent, not a sound was heard. No one spoke a word.

The contestants were getting ready the very next day. Both the participants and the crowd were nervous because it looked like a storm was heading their way.

Tucán announced the rules to make sure everything was fine. All runners must start behind the starting line. You will race through a treacherous maze made of hedges, trees, stone walls, and vines. The maze has very little flaws because Beaver came up with all the designs. The walls were very high, they were so high that birds could fly but not see over the walls. This made the maze a very windy place, the strong winds were loud with howling calls. The gun was shot. All the birds took off without a second thought.

Hummingbird was struggling from the beginning, the announcer stated that Hummingbird wouldn't be winning. The crowd shouted, "There is no proof, you gotta be kidding!" "Let Hummingbird have a chance, I mean we can't predict that far in advance!"

Unfortunately, the winds were just too strong, and Hummingbird flew and flew but couldn't go on. The remaining contestants were moving along. Everyone was cheering for Eagle as he glided, but Raven and Parrot were moving behind, just a little lopsided.

Ostrich was very fast, he did have an advantage by not being affected by the wind, he was glad he was in the race he had decided. Parrot and Raven were moving head to head, but with those strong winds, they collided. Both

Parrot and Raven got a concussion, so the announcer said they had to forfeit, there was no further discussion.

Ostrich and Eagle were both going strong. The crowd was getting nervous about their judgements against Ostrich, and how they were wrong.

Just then there was a loud crack in the sky. The thunder and lightning storm came in a blink of an eye. Eagle was furious, he could not get his wings wet because they became too heavy, and he wouldn't be able to fly. He flew down to the ground, he would have to walk the rest of the way. He didn't like that the weather made him lose that day.

Ostrich ran fast, he was finally going to win at last! Just before the finish line, Ostrich thought this was further than anyone expected, there was no need for Eagle to feel rejected. He ran back to Eagle and asked if they could walk across the finish line together. We both cannot fly, so let's show the others how birds can still be strong in this horrible weather.

Tucan shouted over the intercom, "It looks like we have a tie, and neither bird could even fly! "It looks like even in a competition, you can find an ally."

The crowd all shouted and cried. The birds apologized to Ostrich for making fun of him because of his size. Both Ostrich and Eagle won a prize. Every bird realized that if birds can come together, they can do great things, it's just about the compromise.

Why the brain will hinder when using shoulds and absolutes villains

Speaking in absolutes is deciding in advance a response. It is a way of thinking where you apply one experience to all experiences, including those in the future. When you are making decisions, be careful of people who speak in shoulds and absolutes. When this type of thinking villain is used, you can weaken your reputation and come across as being better then others. Next time, rather than use words like **ALWAYS** and **MUST,** try words more like " usually or I would prefer to."

Absolute words

All, Always, Every, Just, Only, Never, None, No, Not, Must, Should.

Meditation activity

This meditation activity can take anywhere from between one to ten minutes. You can start off with a shorter period of time and extend that as you develop your meditation skills and your confidence:

- Name your current emotion, if you are unsure about what you are feeling; that is okay. It's perfectly normal to feel many things at once, or possibly nothing at all.

- Sit in a relaxing position. Turn off all interruptions. Do you like to sit in the dark or a place with some light?

- Start off by taking three deep breaths, breathing in through your nose and out through your mouth.

- Now think of your favorite color.

- Pretend you are looking at this color for the very first time.

- What is the size and shape of this color? How does it feel: warm, cold, gooey?

- What's its texture: soft, spikey, smooth? Does it make any sounds as you are looking at this color? The ripping of paper, running water, or crinkling of leaves as you walk over them? Lastly, does your color have a taste or smell? Could it taste like your favorite piece of candy or smell like fresh rain?

- Continue to breathe and focus on your favorite color! Now as you continue to think about your color, notice how your body is feeling. If you are having a difficult time sitting still, that's okay. Continue to sit for a few more breaths and say to your body "We are practicing staying calm and still."

When you are ready to get up, open your eyes and notice how your body is feeling. What emotion are you feeling after thinking about your favorite color?

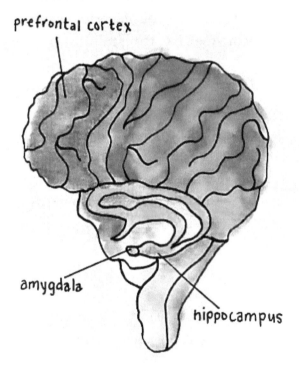

Mindfulness activity

1. The five senses

When experiencing a moment of stress, or as a way to reconnect. Relax and ask yourself:

- What are five things I can see?
- Four things I can touch?
- Three things I can hear?
- Two things I can smell?
- One thing I can taste?

Mindfulness practices can help us to increase our ability to calm emotions, decrease stress, worry and sadness. It can also help us to focus our attention, as well as to observe our thoughts and feelings without judgment.

2. Nostril breathing/cowabunga breathing

An excellent mindfulness activity is nostril breathing also known as cowabunga breathing. You start by blocking one nostril, breathe in for 5, block the other nostril, breathe out for 7.

With regular practice, alternate-nostril breathing can bring better balance to your nervous system and less stress response and activity over time. It lowers blood pressure. Deep breathing and alternate-nostril breathing slow your heartbeat and lower your blood pressure and improves how we feel.

Chapter

12

....

Overgeneralization

....

Ms. Bella

Ms. Bella was such a cute pup, with her curled tail and oversized pointy ears. She set high goals for herself to accomplish, and was very smart, but she had too many fears. Many negative thoughts to her dismay, she became more hopeless each day. Her fears kept her up late, and with little sleep, she was easy to irritate.

Everyday, her list of fears grew and grew: separation from family, speaking in public, loud sounds, public places, heights, and tiny spaces to name a few. These fears were intrusive, her happiness seemed illusive. She began to overgeneralize. She got asked out on a date, but not a second one, her friends had to over sympathize. One bad date does not mean you will never find your true love! That is just unheard of!

She would randomly cry to her disgrace. Her logic thinking skills would leave without a trace. Bella began to believe her emotions were too much to handle so she must take up too much space. Bella wondered if she could ever meet her full potential. Racing thoughts, body pain, upset stomach—they all needed to disappear, that was essential.

A friend recommended talking to a professional, for Bella's small everyday worries were becoming obsessional. Her friend told her:

> "You failed one test so that wasn't your best."

"Now you refuse to come and play because you believe something bad is coming your way. Just because you live in California does not mean an earthquake will happen each day."

"You think you're dumb because of one test outcome. That's like saying you are a pilot since you have been on a plane. . . . Now that's just insane."

"It's going to be okay, you just need to take it day by day. I do suggest that you breathe and rest."

Bella ended up seeing a therapist, who taught her how to reframe. Having negative thoughts was not the end game. By replacing negative thoughts with ones that were more realistic, Bella found her life less fearful and fatalistic.

She was able to go to the vet's without those self-sabotaging and negative threats. It was now just a scary thought when she needed to get a shot. Bella for the first time was able to go to the beach and do some volunteer outreach. She never got in the water, but that was not a bother! Bella still has many fears, but they have calmed down some and every day doesn't end in tears.

Bella has become very aware that she needs to do some self-care. She says it has helped, I swear! Some things she enjoys are yoga, playing fetch, going to the park and drinking wine in Calistoga. Being spiritual or hanging out with friends that have mutual beliefs, or are at least similar. Bella loves listening to music and helping others, she feels altruistic. Having gratitude is helping her cope with dealing with her negative feelings and giving her a much better attitude.

Why the brain becomes biased when using overgeneralization

When the brain is overgeneralizing, we are seeing the world too broad, too simplified, and over reduced.

What is overgeneralization?

Overgeneralization is when a person makes hasty generalizations from insufficient evidence.

Can you identify the cognitive distortions of over-generalization from the sentences below?

1. I failed my math test so I am going to fail all of my tests this week.

2. I love the colors red, orange, yellow, blue, and green so I like most colors in the rainbow.

3. I do not like peaches so I hate fruit.

4. My mom yelled at me so she must hate me.

5. I made one mistake at work, that does not mean I am a bad employee.

6. I traveled to Florida in December, and the weather was perfect; Florida must have perfect weather year round.

7. All larger people overeat and are lazy.

8. I get along with my sister most of the time, we have a pretty good relationship.

9. Smart people do not have to try in school.

10. All depressed people look sad, are lazy, and don't hang out with friends.

Out of these statements, the only ones that are not overgeneralized thinking patterns are 2, 5 and 8.

How to stop overgeneralization

1. Use mindfulness and listen for overgeneralization and notice it happening.
2. See the positives in life to prevent blaming and shaming ourselves and others.
3. Next, stop labeling others and yourself with words like bad and good to prevent hurting yourself and others.
4. Be specific by using smart goals.

COMMON FEARS

1. Hospitals, illnesses and death

2. Things we are allergic to

3. Spiders and insects

4. Public speaking, test taking

5. Disasters

6. Accidents

RESOURCES

National Domestic Violence Hotline 1-800-799-SAFE

National Sexual Assault
   Hotline........................1-800-656-HOPE (4673)

United States Elder Abuse Hotline 1-866-363-4276

National Child Abuse
   Hotline................. 1-800-4-A-CHILD (422-4453)

Eating Disorders Awareness and
   Prevention........................... 1-800-931-2237

Eating Disorders Center................. 1-888-236-1188

National Runaway Switchboard......... 1-800-621-4000

Teenline 1-888-747-TEEN

Youth Crisis Hotline 1-800-448-4663

Alcohol Treatment Referral Hotline
   (24 hours).......................... 1-800-252-6465

Drug Abuse National Helpline 1-800-662-4357

Gay and Lesbian National Hotline....... 1-888-843-4564

Suicide Hotline 1-800-SUICIDE (784-2433)

National Domestic Violence Hotline 1-800-799-SAFE

National Domestic Violence Hotline
   Spanish 1-800-942-6908

Battered Women and their Children 1-800-603-HELP

Mental-Health Crisis Hotline........................ 988

About the Authors

....

Gaelle Carey

....

Gaelle is a Belgian-American licensed marriage family therapist and a licensed vocational nurse. She previously worked in diverse clinical settings such as emergency in-patient care, outpatient mental health clinics, residential facilities, and hospice. Gaelle provides support services to children and their families.

Danielle Ritenour

Danielle is a licensed marriage family therapist who has worked with Gaelle in previous clinical settings, such as outpatient mental health clinics, eating disorder residential facilities, and county-funded programs that work with foster children and their parents. Danielle has also worked in the school districts of both San Diego and San Francisco County. Danielle enjoys her free time at the beach and playing with her dog, Bella. Danielle is a believer in therapy. She also believes in surrounding yourself with people who bring you positivity, things you love, and living by your own values. These are some of the greatest coping skills.

CPSIA information can be obtained
at www.ICGtesting.com
Printed in the USA
LVHW050135050323
740945LV00002B/11